"Captured Chaos"

Terrika

Thank You's

Father, I thank you for everything. I knew I was destined for greatness just didn't know when I'd "arrive." I am so glad that despite my trials and tribulations I didn't give up I went harder. I love who I am becoming. I pray I ma making you proud! Please never take your hands off me! My Messiah!

Angels

To my babies. I love ya'll deeply. Thank you for being patient with me. Remember to always put God first and keep yourselves right after Him. The world will adjust. I know you all can and will do whatever you put your mind to. Remain consistent!

I love you.

Supporters

Thank you all for your support. None of it has gone unnoticed. If I could leave you with anything: "Believe in yourselves that's how you make a believer out of others." Do what makes you happy! Stay tuned!

To myself:

I am very proud of you. You know where you came from and what you faced. I am glad you persevered and didn't allow outside noise to keep you stagnant. You held your own and kept your head when you wanted to lose it and for that you deserve all of the good that you have and that is coming your way! Continue to reach for the stars and know you are touching YOU! I love you, baby!

The Crew

"Lance what was that shit you was telling us we needed to watch from the last time we was round here?" Earl said and kept flickering through the channels and munching on some chips. Janice, Mel, Carl, and Lance were in the kitchen fixing the food to serve for everyone. "I think he said Taken 2 you know he loves some Liam." Janice said. "Yup. There you go. All niggas love Liam. Ya'll know he a nigga at heart?" Earl said. They all laugh. "I got the flick on the tube what ya'll waiting on? Oh, where da hell is O at? Her thick ass!" Earl said and checked his cellphone. He put it on the coffee table. "She said she bout to pull up. Ima tell her you wanna squeeze her fat ass E. Nasty boy!" Mel said. They all laughed. "Shitttt you ain't gotta tell her I'll touch and tell her my damn self." E said. The doorbell rings. "Ohhhh that's slim, thick right dere!" E said and jumped up and ran to the front door. Everyone runs to the kitchen window to see if it is O. "Lawwwdd" she has no idea E here and gone try to pinch her ass. Ya'll memba the last time we was at Chuck house?" Mel was saying and Janice interrupted. "That damn E and the pool water." Janice said and they all laughed. "Dat nigga said Splish splash and rubbed his wet hands all on her ass." Carl said and they all laughed out loud. "Damn, aye turn around right quick." E said and O fell out laughing. "He is sick. Damn girl can't even get in the housed good and he ready to eat her up." Mel said. They all laugh. Everyone starts to take the serving trays full of food into the dining room. They all take turns looking at O and greeting her. If the cookie monster would let me in the damn house, I'd be helping ya'll with the food. Hey family." O said and everyone laughs. As soon as O looks over E's shoulder E moves to block her view. "I got what you looking for right here slim thick." E said. They both laughed. The rest of the crew are putting then food down on the table. Mel walks to the front door. "Ummm E release her and her ass." Mel said. Mel and O laugh. E sucks his teeth. "Go head Mel. Blocking. You clearly see me and bae catching up." E said. Mel grabs O's hand and leads her away from E. He shakes his head and walks away sad. "I'll kick it with you in a few *bae*." O said. E almost breaks his neck turning to look in O's direction. Everyone laughs. They all take turns going into the downstairs bathroom washing their hands. When they finish, they gather at the dining room table. "I'll lead us in prayer." Carl said. They hold hands and bow their heads. "Amen Amen E said and they all laugh. "What? I know The Lord." E said. "Yeah, we know. Especially when you calling on Him after the drinks kick in. Boy you be praising Him some kinda bad." Carl said. "Yeah whatever man." E said and they all laugh. "So, E what's this I hear about some footage you have on me at a pool party? I know you be stalking…I mean capturing my angles and what not but how you gone get the best footage and not share?" O said. They all look at E. "I didn't know he was holding out. Come on E. Share ya shit my guy." Mel said. E excuses himself from the table and goes near the front door where he has a duffle bag at. He rummages through it to find another cellphone. He gras it and holds it up while walking back towards the crew. "The infamous phone." E says. "So, I guess erbody here has a phone for communicating and another for art." Janice said. "Guess so." E said. E starts pulling up different pictures and videos. "Nah, you know we can't see them. You playing now." O said. "I have the tables, why don't we all grab our plates and drinks and go into the living room that way we all can check out what Picasso has." Lance said. They all laugh. "I got yo Picasso nigga. You gone regret that snarky ass comment when you check out what I got." E said. "Trust me I know it's some dope shit. I taught you everything you know." Lance said and they all laughed. "Yeah, you taught me quite a bit but check this out." E said. E has already started sharing his footage on the big screen. Mel was sipping her drink when she stopped suddenly and put her glass down. "Damn, nice scenery. You edited this already E?" Mel asked. "Nah, why?" E said. "Cause this shit is legit." Mel said. "Thanks." E said. "You're welcome." Mel said. "Aye, E put that audio in there from last week. Remember the sounds we were sampling from that cookout?" Lance said. "Oh yeah. I gotcha." E said. E changed the audio and started the footage over and created a flipogram. Everyone was amazed at what he was sharing. Mel got up and told him to share some of what she captured when she and the ladies hung out at a lounge a week prior. "Mel, I hope you not sharing all of the shit we have in your phone." Janice said and covered her face. The ladies laughed. "We fam ain't nobody in here gone judge ya'll. What ya'll had ya'll titties out or something?" Carl asked. E looked directly at O. "Nah, nothing like that. But sometimes we can get down." O said and she blew a kiss at E. E was grinning too hard. He started to rub his own nipples and caught her imaginary kiss. Everyone started laughing. "Boy, focus." Mel said. They all laughed and looked up to the big screen. "Ok, Mel let me find out. I be thinking you not capturing my good side but damn. You got it Sis. Thank you. Got me out here looking like a fucking model." Janice said.

"Everyone was looking at the screen in amazement. "I be playing around but I think we should see what Carl got. Carl, the Diner. I know we were cutting up that day, but I don't remember ever seeing footage. Oh, and ya'll know we were cute. As per usual. Share!" Mel said. Carl gets up quickly and says: Oh, damn. You right. I just be playing for real. Ya'll the OG'S." Carl goes into another room and grabs his bag. He brings it back into the living room with the crew. "I guess it's safe to say we all bring our equipment just in case. Cause erbody brought a bag of tricks." Janice said. Everyone laughs. "Yeah, I have a backpack in the trunk. I will not be the only one without footage. I learned my lesson when we went out of town on a whim." O said. "Oh, my goodness. You were a pissy mess the entire weekend. We had so many pictures and videos. You didn't have shit in your phone O. It was crazy. And the water scenes. OMG they were to die for." Mel said. "Don't remind me. I was sick." O said and laughed. "Look at this." Carl said and pointed at the big screen. Everyone sat up straight in their chairs and their eyes were on bulge. "Carl! Wow. When did you get these?" O asked. "Umm. It was a few events I put together. Like I have plenty of footage of each event. But when I started playing one night when I couldn't sleep man I couldn't resist. And I added some audio on some of not but not all because I wanted to chime in on us talking and laughing. That's what made this shit more live." Carl said. "I feel you on that. I was reading something the other day about submitting footage. I can't remember if it was just for pics or videos, but I'll look into it later and put it in the chat. I know if there are any contests we gone win them shits cause just one of us has enough shit to shake the universe up. I mean we be lit and our footage be outta this world." Lance said. "Hol up. O what was that talent something you were telling us about that one time with your job? I can't remember what exactly you said but remember the luncheon and our pics being included and someone said something about cash prizes?" Mel asked O. "Oh, yeah. Melvin been talking me to death about our pics too. My job was introducing new software and used my cellphone and our pix for the showcase. I didn't think anything on it. Well, I was told somebody used them for a campaign advertisement too. Hmmm. Let me send a text and see if they can email me that footage my job put together. Cause wait til ya'll see it. It was nice." O said. O started to text her co-worker. Before she could send another text, she received a phone call. She excused herself from everyone and walked into the kitchen to talk. "Hey, it's O." E was watching her the entire time. "I think I should go ahead and get my bag huh?" Janice said. "Yeah, cause you have the most laid back footage of us. From the cooking, decorating, and just chilin vibes. Oh, my goodness, Janice, remember Stacey's baby shower? That footage was too cute." Mel said. "Oh yeah. Let me get my shit and share. Cause I'm sitting here stuffing my face feeling my ass spread like butter." Janice said and laughed. She takes one last bite and jumps up. Carl sips his drink and laughs. Shaking his head he pauses the footage on the screen. "I think we should really start creating compilations. Look at what we've shared so far." Carl says. "Yeah, you might be on to something. I know we can enter our footage into some contests or something and get rich. Shit the amount of fun we be having and people be photobombing our shit all the time." Mel said. "They really do." E said. "Contests though? I heard Pharrell doing something in Hampton Roads. Not sure exactly what but we love a road trip." Janice said as she walked back into the living room digging in her bags. "Hey, can you plug me up? I got some stuff. It's not as wild but." Janice said. "Gotcha. I know ya'll got a few titty clips somewhere. Just joking." Carl said. E quickly looked in O's direction and started cheezin. O started walking back into the living room and all eyes were on her. "What? Why ya'll looking at me weird?" O said. They all started laughing. "You don't want to know." Mel said. "You are probably right." O said and laughed. She sat down and smiled. Carl hooked up Janice's footage and they all were smiling hard watching how he was playing the video and making edits. "When we finish watching this Carl can you put this on the big screen next? Skateboard P has some event coming up. If ya'll down let's go and make history. I can reach out to KK and get us some more equipment. Hell, she might wanna come too. Oh, this gone be legendary." Janice said. Everyone agrees and starts chatting. "Wow, Janice, I didn't know you got all of this from the baby shower. You really dope Sis. Damn!" Mel said. "Yeah, girl. You should be entering your stuff into some contests. All of ya'll should. We really could be doing some big stuff. Damn, while I'm saying all of this. Let me text my cousin. Ya'll remember last summer when we were the first ones on the scene of that house fire?" O said. Everyone started chiming in and laughing. "Oh, shit. I forgot about that." E said. "How could you forget. Shit was hilarious. Carl was still drunk as shit, and you got his ass. Close up!" O said. "Well, I could send it to my cousin as to the radio station. He's doing a lil podcast now…" O was saying. "Not you two." Janice said. "Me too what?" "Saying a lil…that blows me." Janice said. They all started laughing.

"Ya'll know what I meant." O said. "Luckily, we know who you are. So, you mean no harm when you say lil anything. You are forgiving. I'm still gone tell him." Janice said and they all laughed. "Yeah, this can be like the anniversary of and the fact that we got the footage. Oh, Carl you gotta edit it just right." O said. "Gotcha." Carl said. "We really out here living our best lives and capturing our chaos." E said. "Chaos to us but *we had a time last night* to some." Mel said. They all laugh. Everyone starts to place their flash drives on the coffee table and Carl starts to play and edit their footage. They watched all of the memories they have created thus far for hours.

Stacey's Birthday Party

"Hey Stace! Happy Birthday chick." E said. The Crew started walking towards Stacey's backyard. "Thanks E. I'm glad ya'll made it. The footage on Chi's podcast was the shit. I hope ya'll bought your cameras cause it's gone be a full house. Get everything. Cause I'ma show my ass tonight." Stacey said and they all started laughing. As they enter her backyard, they wave at everyone and take turns hugging Stacey. "Ya'll can take your bags in the guest room on the first floor. E knows where it is. I'm bout to get round 2 started." Stacey said and held up her glass. "Girl, let me hurry up and catch up with you." O said. E smiles at O and everyone starts to laugh. "Don't go too far." E said. "What?" O said and started to walk away fast. They all laugh out loud. As O and Stacey are walking off Stacey whispers: "Girl he still stuck on you? Stalk much?" They both laugh and walk inside. "I can't wait to see what footage we get tonight. This gone be fun. I heard Ella gone be here. That fool knows how to party." Mel said. "Aye remember when she got into it with that bartender then went behind the counter and started fixing our drinks?" Mel said. Nigga. Do I." Carl said. "Ya girl didn't budge when security came either." Janice said. "Shit. She bigger than the big niggas. Well, them hips are lethal." Carl said. They all laughed. "She official tho!" Mel said. "Yeah, she is solid." Janice said. So many guests started to arrive, and Mel and The Crew have been snapping pictures and recording them as they enter the back yard. They are making sure they are not missing a thing. Stacey grabs the microphone from the DJ stand and starts speaking to everyone: "Aye, I know we just getting started but grab somebody and make them feel loved. I mean really loved. Cause life is short and ain't no need for any of us to be alone or lonely. This next song is for me and my booski. I love you babe, thank you in advance for tonight!" Stacey gives the Mic back to the DJ and walks towards her Boo. He greets her with open arms. They kiss and start slow dancing as soon as the next song spins. The Crew started to playfully dance with one another. None of them have ever messed around. They have genuine love for one another and wouldn't dare test the friendship like that. Just as the party was starting the crew started to capture everything. From dancing, singing, hugs, laughter, drinking, eating, and chit chatting. They are not about to miss an opportunity. The hours pass by faster than they could imagine, and they are still enjoying one another's company. Stacey has since then crashed on her couch and her boo is not far behind. As people are leaving in the wee hours of the morning the crew is making their rounds to collect footage of the party and are whispering about their edits. Giggles and whispers meet them at the front door.

Skateboard P

The Crew are piled up at Carl's house getting ready to attend the event at The

Oceanfront in Virginia Beach. "So, we really bout to be a part of Pharrell's concert? Damn, all those pix and videos and here we are. I knew we could, but just didn't know when. I just want to thank ya'll for seeing this through. Does everyone have their batteries and back-ups?" Carl asked. The Crew all responded saying yes. "I am so excited. A few more minutes and I think we're ready." Janice said. She and the rest of the women are looking in his mirror in his living room and making sure their make-up is on point. "I know we gone blow their minds." E said. "Oh, yeah. Let's pray before we go ya'll. God blessed us with these gifts, what we're going to do with them is our gift to Him." O said.

Everyone gathers, holds hands, and begin to pray. The finish getting ready. Their things are already packed in their vehicles. They head out to the concert.

They arrived at The Oceanfront. They are met by guards, police, and some of Pharrell's crew. They are helped with their belongings. Their smiles are huge, and they are being asked what they want to eat and drink on during the show. Treated like celebrities, they are taken aback. Just as they are stepping up on the stage, the curtains drawn, they see Pharrell. They are holding back showing too much excitement. As he is talking to someone about his set one of his crew members points to The Crew. "Hey, ya'll. I am so glad you all could make it." Pharrell says and walks towards them. They embrace each other with handshakes and hugs. Mel begins to take pictures of all of them and Pharrell has someone play music so they can loosen up and build a rapport. After a few moments of creating new memories one of his people gets his attention and he excuses himself. The Crew are gawking over the videos and pictures they just got.

They are next up to hit the stage and capture Pharrell and the concert in its entirety! They have so much footage, more than enough to last a lifetime. The two hour show Pharrell put on was more than amazing. After the show and after party they hung out with Pharrell and his some of his close friends exchanging the pictures and watching the footage. As Carl begins to edit some of the videos Pharrell introduces Carl to one of his right-hand men and gets the crew together to discuss their new careers moving forward. A deal was made, and magic was born.

The Crew is now working as Pharrell's posse. They travel near and far capturing his most intimate moments and his stardom.

Who could have known a few pictures would lead them to such lucrative careers?!! The risk worth taking is in the unknown.